How To Manage Teams
The No Waffle Guide To Managing Your Team Effectively

I0484446

Copyright © 2014 by Louise Palmer.

All rights reserved. No part of this publication may be reproduced, distributed, or transmitted in any form or by any means, including photocopying, recording, or other electronic or mechanical methods, without the prior written permission of the publisher, except in the case of brief quotations embodied in critical reviews and certain other noncommercial uses permitted by copyright law.

Table of Contents

Effective Managers

Different Management Styles

Managers can be task-orientated and/or person-orientated. Task-orientated managers focus on managing and completing the tasks that are assigned to the team. Person-orientated managers focus on managing the people who carry out the work. Whilst it depends on the environment as to which approach is best, in general, there usually needs to be a focus on both.

There are different management styles including transactional, transformational and laissez-faire.

Transactional Management Style

A manager who uses a transactional style sets goals for the team. If these goals are achieved, they receive rewards. These are considered 'transactions'. Managers tend to leave the team to complete their tasks and only get involved in there appears to be a problem. A transactional manager will spend time ensuring these transactions are completed successfully rather than providing true leadership. Most leaders and managers will need to use transactional management to some extent.

Transformational

Transformational management is more inspirational. Managers encourage their team to become involved and share thoughts and ideas. Managers take the time to provide formal and informal recognition for achievements. This type of manager encourages their team to be creative. They articulate a vision of the future and act as a role model that people wish to recreate in themselves. This type of management naturally motivates people.

Laissez-faire

This type of manager avoids making decisions and does not actively manage their team. They prefer to leave their team to get on with their work, even if there is clearly a need for them to get involved. Laissez-faire managers may be lacking in confidence, wish to avoid confrontation or lack the managerial skills required.

In some situations a Laissez-Faire style of management can be appropriate. It can encourage individuals and teams to solve their own problems and promotes autonomy. However, if a laissez-faire manager fails to take control of their team when it is required, it can hinder the team's success.

Situational Management

Different workplace situations require different management styles. Effective managers recognise this and adapt their management style accordingly (Hershey and Blanchard 1969). Solely relying on one management style can lead to poorly performing teams.

Do you manage the individuals in your team differently? Does their level of confidence, ability to complete tasks and attitude towards the task affect how you subsequently manage them?

Telling/Directing

If an employee has low commitment, low competence, is unable, unwilling, or insecure and lacks confidence, you should take a telling/directing approach. There needs to be a high task focus and low relationship focus.

You can aim to provide clear information on what is expected of the employee both in terms of the job and their conduct. You may try to discover the reason for the lack of motivation and enquire whether the employee needs further training or support. If you focus too much on the relationship, the employee may become confused as the boundaries feel blurred and they may begin to believe they do not have to do all the tasks required of them. It is important you provide clear task based instructions in this situation.

Selling/Coaching

When the employee has a degree of competence and perhaps is over-confident about their abilities, instructing them as to what to do, can reduce their motivation or lead to resistance.

You need to portray another way of working and sell its advantages. You need to create conversations around the tasks ensuring they actively listen. You may decide to use coaching to help this development process.

Participating/Support

When the employee is competent of the tasks required, yet is failing to complete them in a timely manner, you need to understand why. Once you know the reasons, you can try to address these to encourage the employee to complete the tasks as expected.

Employees cannot use their lack of ability as an excuse and you need to focus on motivation issues. It can help to praise the individual when they achieve the tasks required of them.

Delegating/Observing

When the employee is both competent and motivated, you can leave them to autonomously achieve the task. It is important that you still occasionally check their work to ensure they are maintaining their usual high standards.

An employee who is willing and able to complete their tasks with little intervention will need far less managerial input. However, it is important not to ignore the efforts and successes of these individuals as this could eventually lead to a lack of motivation. Regularly provide praise to ensure they feel valued and appreciated.

Attributes of Successful Managers

Research shows the following aspects contribute to long lasting success in high level executives (Eichinger and Lombardo 2004):

1. Intelligence
2. Technical/Operational Ability
3. Motivation
4. Experience
5. People Skills
6. Learning Abilities

1. Intelligence

In lower level roles, intelligence can impact on whether an employee is a poor or high performer. In senior level roles most executives have an adequate level of IQ. They have needed to demonstrate their intelligence in order to attain their current job role and therefore intelligence is not likely to predict whether a manager will be a poor or high performer.

A previously successful manager may start to struggle in a more senior role if they are unable to demonstrate Emotional Intelligence. Emotional Intelligence refers to how good they are with people.

2. Technical/Operational Ability

Technical and operational competence includes the executive's technical knowledge and ability to complete tasks successfully. It is not usually a large differentiator in the higher level jobs. This is because, like IQ, they have had to demonstrate a certain level of competence in order to achieve their current position.

3. Motivation

Usually those in senior manager roles have high levels of ambition. This ambition has provided them with the motivation to achieve their current position. As most high level managers possess high levels of motivation, it is not a differentiator between successful and non successful executives.

Intelligence, Technical/Operational ability and Motivation levels often impact on performance and differentiate workers in lower level positions. The levels of these elements are usually high in executives and are therefore not a differentiating predictor over which executives will enjoy long term success.

4. Experience

The types of experience a manager has had may impact on whether or not they are successful. These experiences might include previous management experience, their experience of being managed, seeing a project through from beginning to end, events of success, events of failure, problem solving and learning opportunities.

5. People Skills

The manager's ability to manage their own emotions, as well as other's emotions, is a predictor of management success. Lombardo and Eichinger (2003) state that people skills account for 6 out of the top 10 reasons for derailment. These include over managing, insensitivity, defensiveness, arrogance, the failure to build teams, and lack of composure. . It is important that a manager is able to manage their own emotions and the emotions of others. This is referred to as Emotional Intelligence (Goleman 1999). We will look at Emotional Intelligent management qualities shortly.

6. Learning Abilities

A key factor for management success is learning agility. Executives who derail view their learning to be complete. Whereas successful executives differ in that they tend to view learning as a continuous process. They are continually looking for new methods, better ways of working, alternative ways to think and they experiment with fresh approaches to old tasks.

Successful executives are motivated by their desire to educate themselves which enables them to make informed decisions and take considered risks. If they are faced with a problem which they do not have the knowledge or skills to solve, they conduct research and experiment with possible solutions until they achieve success. Learning agility is a large contributing factor to whether or not a manager will be successful.

Management and Emotional Intelligence

As already stated Emotional Intelligence (Goleman 1998) is a very important aspect of management success. Emotional Intelligence consists of a number of competencies. These include personal competencies and social competencies. Personal competencies relate to your ability to manage your own emotions. Social competencies relate to your ability to manage emotions in others.

The table below demonstrates the separate elements of Personal Competencies and Social Competencies.

Personal Competencies	Social Competencies
Self Awareness: Understanding the self.	**Social Awareness:** Awareness of other people's emotions, needs and anxieties.
Self Management: Management of emotions and desires. Emotional capabilities that aid goal achievement.	**Relationship Management:** Ability to evoke desired responses from other people.

Those managers who demonstrate high levels of emotional intelligence consistently outperform managers with lower levels of emotional intelligence. The competencies of a highly emotionally intelligent manager are listed below. As you read each competency, consider whether it highlights any development areas for you and whether you would like to address these.

PERSONAL COMPETENCE

SELF-AWARENESS

Emotional self-awareness. Managers high in emotional self-awareness are aware of their feelings and how they impact on others and their job performance. They are aware of their values and how these influence their actions. They are able to see the whole picture. They embrace both negative and positive feelings. They feel motivated and driven to achieve their goals.

Accurate self-assessment. Managers with high self-awareness know their strengths and limitations. They work to continually identify development areas and are open to receiving constructive feedback. They are comfortable enough to laugh at themselves. They are at ease asking for help and aware of what they need to do to further improve their performance.

Self-confidence. Managers high in self-confidence are able to accurately assess their strengths and abilities. They exhibit confidence with challenging tasks and projects. They display self-assurance.

PERSONAL COMPETENCE

SELF-MANAGEMENT

Self-control. Managers with the ability to demonstrate self-control are in command of their negative emotions. They channel them into positive outcomes. A manager with self-control stays calm during a crisis or if under stress. They remain calm and collected whatever the situation.

Transparency. Managers who demonstrate transparency talk freely with others regarding their emotions, thoughts, beliefs, values and actions. They are honest about their mistakes or faults. If they disapprove of another individual's actions, they will take considered action.

Adaptability. Managers with high adaptability are comfortable with constant change. They are able to work with multiple demands and keep their focus and energy throughout. They are comfortable with new ways of working.

Achievement. Managers who demonstrate high achievement levels set challenging, yet realistic, goals for themselves and their teams. They have a strong motivation and drive to achieve these goals. They encourage others who are lacking motivation. They ensure work is of a high standard. They evaluate risk accurately. They are driven to learn and encourage others to do the same.

Initiative. A manager high in initiative creates and seeks opportunities rather than waiting for them to present themselves as a result of circumstance. They strive to achieve positive change for the future.

Optimism. Managers high in optimism will look for opportunities in setbacks. They view others in a positive light and expect people to do their best. They are driven to create a positive working environment. They expect a positive future and work to make it a reality.

SOCIAL COMPETENCE

SOCIAL AWARENESS

Empathy. Managers who demonstrate empathy are able to read emotions in others and react appropriately. They ensure they actively listen to individuals, taking time to fully comprehend the other person's perspective. Their empathy makes it easy for them to build relationships with others from diverse backgrounds and cultures.

Organizational awareness. A manager with organizational awareness is able to look beyond formal job titles and analyse who really holds the most power. They understand crucial social networks and political aspects. They are aware of written and non-written rules that exist within the organisation.

Service. Managers high in the service competence regularly evaluate client satisfaction to ensure they are delivering the best service possible and meeting the client's needs. They encourage and foster an emotional climate to encourage positive interactions and relationships with clients.

SOCIAL COMPETENCE

RELATIONSHIP MANAGEMENT

Inspiration. Managers who inspire can liaise with others to develop a joint vision of the ideal future. They ensure that individual and team goals link to the overall goals of the organisation. They only ask others to do tasks that they would do themselves. They are passionate about the vision they create which encourages others to go beyond their required tasks in order to achieve the vision.

Influence. Managers who are successful at influencing others are persuasive and engaging. They understand how to influence people on an individual basis and this helps them to get buy in from key people.

Developing others. Managers who are effective at developing others feel motivated to help individuals achieve their full potential. They take into account the individual's capabilities and development areas. They take the time to provide regular positive and constructive feedback. They act as coaches and mentors to help individuals and teams reach their full potential.

Change catalyst. Managers who can act as change catalysts identify the need for change. They are able to communicate this need to others and gain support for the changes. They are able to maintain motivation during the change period and overcome any resistance.

Conflict management. Managers who are able to manage conflicts successfully ensure they take the time to listen to both parties' perspectives and fully understand the situation. They facilitate discussions between the parties and encourage them to keep statements task focused. They encourage the parties to work together to discover possible solutions to the task based conflict.

Teamwork and collaboration. Managers who are good team players are helpful and co-operative. They provide appropriate support and ensure they are involved with the tasks. They create a collective atmosphere as the whole team works towards the same goals and vision. They are able to develop close relationships with their team members that often go beyond work obligations.

You should by now have a good picture of what makes a successful manager. Let's contrast this to flaws that can derail managers. Zenger and Folkman (2009) conducted a management study using 360 degree surveys on 450, Fortune 500 executives. They then analysed the 11 000 least effective managers. They found these ineffective managers all had one or more of the following shortcomings:

- Lack of motivation
- Satisfied with their own average performance
- Did not hold a clear vision of the desired future
- Demonstrated poor judgements
- Were not keen to collaborate with others
- Did not act as a positive role model for others to follow
- Resisted change and new ideas
- Unable to amend behaviour after negative outcomes
- Low interpersonal skill level
- Did not further develop other people's skills

Interestingly the ineffective managers were unaware they exhibited these behaviours. Those who were rated the most negatively, rated themselves substantially more positively than the ratings they received. This demonstrates how important it is for managers to actively seek feedback from others.

Look back through the book so far and see if you can identify any areas that you think you could improve as a manager.

Create a list of action points you would like to address. Consider how you can improve your skills. You might choose workshops, online training courses, books, or internet research.

Managing Teams

When leading teams it is useful to identify the different personalities and working preferences of your team members. There are various tools we can use to help us identify the various aspects of a team.

Team Personalities

You may have heard of the Myers Briggs Type Indicator (MBTI). It is a tool which is used to assess different personality types. It highlights people's different psychological preferences and their perceptions of the world. It also identifies how people prefer to make decisions.

Below is a brief summary of the different personality types.

Introversion and Extraversion

People either lean towards introversion or extraversion when they make decisions.

Introversion
Thinks things through to reach a conclusion
Contemplates
Believes and understands
Thinks first, acts later
Seeks privacy
Concentrates on thoughts

Extraversion
Talks things through to reach a conclusion
Does
Shows
Acts first, thinks later
Seeks interaction
Thinks 'out loud'

Sensing and iNtuition

People are either sensing or intuitive in style when they consider information.

Sensing
Looks for facts
Acquires details first, then works out bigger picture
Enjoys present
Tends towards realism
Uses what's there
Uses trusted solutions
What is real

iNtuition
Looks for possibilities
Acquires overview first then looks at possibilities
Looks forward to the future
Tends towards idealism
Changes what's there
Creates own solutions
What might be

Thinking and Feeling

People are either thinking or feeling in how they make decisions.

Thinking
Decides using impersonal logic
True v False
Right v Wrong
Detached objectivity
Logical analysis and criticism
Organises
Detached

Feeling

Decides using subjective values

Likes v Dislikes

Good v Bad

Personal involvement

Sympathy and appreciation

Involved

Judging and Perceiving

People are either judging or perceptive in how they like to make final decisions and conduct the necessary activities.

Judging

Makes decision

Seeks closure

Plans and controls life

Structures

Prefers time to spare

Prefers things to be settled

Does task in hand

Perceiving

Acquires information

Maintains openness

Goes with the flow

Meanders

Last minute

Prefers change

Likes to explore all the opportunities the task presents

Go back through the MBTI psychological preferences and make a note of which describes you best:

Introversion or Extraversion?

Sensing or iNtuition?

Thinking or Feeling?
Judging or Perceiving?

Then take the first letter of each and you will have a four letter MBTI type. Note that for iNtuition, you would use the letter N. (This is just to introduce you to the concept and in no way replaces having your MBTI done professionally.)

Next, do this for a few members of your team.

What would likely happen if you were to have two opposites within your team, such as an ESTJ and an INFP?

How could knowing this help you to work more efficiently with your team?

Comment

If you had one team member that was an ESTJ and another team member who was an INFP, they may experience frustration with each other. The ESTJ type would likely want final decisions made and plans created. The INFP would prefer things to be more flexible and undecided. There are many different conflicts these two personality types could experience.

Work tasks can be designed to take into consideration people's differing personality traits. In addition, the understanding that friction is arising from these differences can in itself result in improved team cohesion.

MBTI and Problem Solving in Teams

When teams are working to solve problems, you can ask questions which appeal to either Sensing or Intuitive personality types.

Sensing: Ask questions about what is actually happening or has happened.
What are the facts?
What is the situation as it stands?
What has been tried before?
What has worked?

What has not worked?

What are the bottom line realities?

What resources do we have available?

Intuitive: Ask questions to discover prospects and potential possibilities.

What could we achieve?

What options do we have?

Can we look at this from another perspective?

What do the facts imply?

Does this issue relate to other issues we are experiencing?

Are there any patterns emerging?

When problem solving in teams, you can also satisfy both the Thinking and the Feeling personality types.

Thinking: Ask questions which evaluate each option.

What are the pros and cons of each option?

Are these options realistic?

Is there a risk to us if we do not act?

How do the options relate to our priorities?

Feeling: Ask questions which evaluate the emotive impact.

Is it in line with our values?

What impact will it have on the team?

What impact will it have on our customers?

Will it impact on work/life balance?

Will people need additional support?

Belbin Team Roles

Another useful tool for managing teams is Belbin's Team Roles. This tool helps you to understand the role each person naturally plays within your team. A team may not be effective because there is a vacant position that nobody naturally takes. This vacant role needs to be assigned to a team member/s. The roles include Plant, Resource-investigator, Co-ordinator,

Shaper, Monitor-evaluator, Team worker, Implementer, Completer Finisher, Specialist.

The table below details each of these roles.

Team Role	Contribution
Plant	Creative, imaginative, innovative.
Resource Investigator	Explores different opportunities, networks with external contacts and conducts research.
Co-ordinator	Formalises goals, encourages final decisions, encourages everyone's involvement.
Shaper	Works hard to overcome obstacles.
Monitor, evaluator	Considers all possible options, effectively evaluates.
Team Worker	Astute, insightful, diplomatic, emotionally supportive.
Implementer	Practical, task focused, considers finer details.
Completer Finisher	Ensures tasks completed in timely manner, develops in-depth plans for group tasks
Specialist	Provides specialist knowledge and skills.

Consider which roles your team members take. Are there any roles that are not currently filled by a team member? If so, does this role need to be allocated to a particular person?

Emotional Intelligence in Teams

eams which demonstrate high levels of Emotional Intelligence outperform teams with lower Emotional Intelligence (Goleman 1999). Highly emotionally intelligent teams are those where the individuals are good at managing their own emotions and others within the team. A highly emotionally intelligent team works cohesively and effectively. Research conducted by Druskat and Wolff (2001) identified norms that resulted in highly emotionally intelligent teams.

Norms – Individual Level

1. The team should be aware if a member is not on the same emotional wavelength. They need to acknowledge any negative statements. Doing so can make a person feel attended to and lessen the intensity of the negative emotion.

2. Time needs to be taken to consider different perspectives.

3. The team needs to consider each team member's thoughts on a task or situation. They need to specifically ask quiet members if they do not voluntarily contribute.

4. . If a concern is raised, it is important the team listens to the concern. The consequences of possible solutions should also be considered. Caution should be exercised when deciding a solution based on the majority vote.

5. Behaviour which crosses the line needs to be confronted. This can be achieved in a light-hearted manner.

Norms – Group Level

1. Teams need to self-evaluate their strengths and weaknesses. The team should celebrate goal achievement. They should actively encourage both positive and constructive feedback on work tasks in order to continually improve performance.

2. Team members should address any aspects of individual or team behaviour which may negatively affect team performance such as conflicts within the team. The effective team will then work to overcome this.

3. Teams need to favour optimism and focus on positive aspects rather than negative ones. Members need to be aware that their emotions, both

positive and negative, are contagious. Even in difficult situations, they need to consider what they can do with the resources available.

Norms - Emotions Outside the Group

1. The team needs to develop positive rapport and relationships with external teams. They may work to create opportunities for networking outside of the group.

2. The team needs to consider external team's needs, perceptions, thoughts and emotions. They can provide support to other teams and invite relevant individuals to attend team meetings.

3. Time should be taken to understand if the proposed actions are congruent with the organisations' culture and politics.

Use these Norms to answer the following questions.

Qu 1. A team have been informed that their head office have decided to integrate a new computer system. This means that all employees will need to attend a 5 day training course. One member of the team is clearly unhappy with the change. Make a note of what impact the following activities would have short and long term. Which option demonstrates the most emotional intelligence?

Option 1: Ignore their behaviour.
Option 2: Ask the team member what their concerns are.
Option 3: Ask the team member what their concerns are and work together to identify solutions.

Comment
Option 3 demonstrates the most emotional intelligence.

Qu 2. A member of the team is regularly taking an hour for lunch when only 30 minutes is permitted. Make a note of what impact the following activities would have short and long term. Which option demonstrates the most emotional intelligence?

Option 1: Joke about their lengthy lunch breaks in front of the team in the hope they will feel embarrassed and only take 30 minutes in future.

Option 2: Make no comment regarding their long lunch breaks.

Option 3: Take them to one side and ask what is making them take longer lunch breaks. Remind them that the rest of their team members are only taking 30 minutes and ask them to do the same.

Comment
Option 3 demonstrates the most emotional intelligence.

Qu 3. A team member has to change their normal shift in order to cover the absence of a colleague. They have had to cancel personal plans and arrive at the office in a clearly agitated state. Make a note of what impact the following activities would have short and long term. Which option demonstrates the most emotional intelligence?

Option 1: Apologise for the situation.

Option 2: When they arrive, publicly thank them for cancelling their plans and coming into the office at such short notice.

Option 3: Try to ignore their agitation.

Comment
demonstrates the most emotional intelligence.

Qu 4. A team have been working hard on a presentation for a client's project. The client did not like the ideas presented to them and is considering taking their custom elsewhere. The team usually enjoys positive feedback from clients and as a result of the meeting are feeling deflated and de-motivated. Make a note of what impact the following activities would have short and long term. Which option demonstrates the most emotional intelligence?

Option 1: The manager raises concerns over the quality of the team's ideas and presentation.

Option 2: The manager avoids talking about the situation with the team.

Option 3: The manager calls a meeting and reminds the team that he believes them to be competent. He works with the team to consider possible solutions with the hope of trying to retain the client.

Comment
Option 3 demonstrates the most emotional intelligence..

Now look back over your notes regarding the impact of the different activities in the short and long term. What do you notice about the short and long term impact of **not** working in an emotionally intelligent way?

What do you notice about the short and long term impact of working in an emotionally intelligent way?

Comment
Some managerial actions may have little impact in the short term, however if repeated over time, they can have negative consequences for the team. Team cohesion can be affected.

A manager who continually demonstrates high levels of emotional intelligence, will ensure that his team works well together and performs to the best of their ability in both the short and long term.

Team Working Behaviours

Social Loafing

If a number of individuals work together as a team, there is a risk of 'Social Loafing'. Research has shown that as the number of people working on a task increases, the effort and/or performance from each person often reduce (Latane at al 1979).

This can be avoided if each person feels that their contribution can be identified and that their contribution makes a significant difference to the overall group achievement of the task (Kerr and Bruun 1983).

Groupthink

You will also need to be aware of group think. When working in groups the desire for unanimity and agreement takes over the clear evaluation of different options (Janis 1972). Other factors such as who holds power and self-esteem issues can also impact on group decisions.

It can be useful to review decisions in a few days time, to give individual members time to evaluate the different options on their own.

References

Belbin, R.M. (1993). Team Roles at Work: A Strategy for Human Resource Management. Oxford: Butterworth-Heinemann.

Druskat, V. U., & Wolff, S. B. (2001). Group Emotional Competence and its Influence on Group effectiveness. In Cary Cherniss and Daniel Goleman (Eds.), Goleman, D. (1999). Working with Emotional Intelligence. Bloomsbury Publishing.

Eichinger, R.W. and Lombardo, M. M. (2004). The 6 Qs of Management: A Blueprint for Enduring Success at the Top. Lominger, The Management Architects.

Finkelstein, S. (2003). Why Smart Executive Fail: And What You Can Learn From Their Mistakes. Portfolio.

Hersey, P. and Blanchard, K. H. (1969). Life Cycle Theory of Management. Training and Development Journal, Vol, 23, Issue 5, 26–34.

Janis, I, L. (1972). Groupthink. Boston. MA: Houghton Mifflin.

Kerr,N.L and Bruun, S.E. (1983) Dispensability of Member Effort and Group Motivation Losses: Free-rider Effects. Journal of Personality and Social Psychology, Vol. 44, pp.78-94.

Latane, B., Williams, K. and Harkins, S. (1979) Many Hands Make Light Work: The Causes and Consequences of Social Loafing. Journal of Personality and Social Psychology, Vol. 37, pp.822-832.

Meindl, J.R., Ehrlich, S.B. and Dukerich, J.M. (1985). The Romance of Management. Administrative Science Quarterly, Vol. 30, pp. 78-102.

Myers, Isabel Briggs; Mary H. McCaulley (1985). Manual: A Guide to the Development and Use of the Myers-Briggs Type Indicator (2nd ed.). Palo Alto, CA: Consulting Psychologists Press.

Zenger, J. and Folkman, J. (2009). Ten Fatal Flaws that Derail Managers. Harvard Business Review.

More books by this author

Change Management for Managers: The No Waffle Guide to Managing Change in the Workplace

Presentation Skills: Portraying Confidence, Answering Tricky Questions and Structuring Content

How to Manage People: The No Waffle Guide to Managing Performance, Change and Stress in the Workplace

How to Manage Stress in the Workplace: The No Waffle Guide for Managers (EBook Only)

Manager's Guide to Providing Feedback: The No Waffle Guide to Providing Feedback and Rewards (EBook Only)

Coaching Skills for Managers: The No Waffle Guide to Getting the Best from Your Team (EBook Only)

What Other Marketing Books Won't Tell You: A Brutally Honest Account of Marketing a Small Business

The Counselling Sessions: Overcoming Feelings of Irritability and Anger in Relationships

The Counselling Sessions: Overcoming Anxiety and Panic Attacks

The Counselling Sessions: Overcoming Low Mood and Depression

www.ingramcontent.com/pod-product-compliance
Lightning Source LLC
Chambersburg PA
CBHW070758180526
45168CB00004B/1670